UNKNOWN FATHER
LOST MOTHER

By
Florinda Gamez

Order this book online at www.trafford.com
or email orders@trafford.com

Most Trafford titles are also available at major online book retailers.

Printed in Victoria, BC, Canada.

ISBN: 978-1-4269-2080-6

*Our mission is to efficiently provide the world's finest, most
comprehensive book publishing service, enabling every author to
experience success. To find out how to publish your book, your way, and
have it available worldwide, visit us online at www.trafford.com*

Trafford rev. 1/19/10

North America & international
toll-free: 1 888 232 4444 (USA & Canada)
phone: 250 383 6864 ♦ fax: 812 355 4082

PART 1
UNKNOWN FATHER, LOST MOTHER

I can remember through the years that I have seen my poor mother lost and lonely more than she had been daring. She had told me when I was about 14 years old, that she got pregnant with me when she was 36 years old. She was deeply in love with my estranged father who she said had died when I was about five years old. I was always looking from a distance at some little girl holding her father's hand walking by proud and happy. But I had to look around most of the times for my mom nowhere to be found. She would always tell me that she was working, and that was most of my childhood years up until I was about 11 or 12. My mother immigrated from Mexico when she found out she was pregnant because my grandparents would never forgive her. She said that her parents and my father's parents were always fighting over loose horses or cattle grazing on their land or vice versa. My mother, Maria decided to cross the border at Brownsville, Texas not knowing she would deliver before Christmas of 1949. My mother would always tell me a story about her getting all dressed up and ready to go grocery shopping. Even if it was just going around the corner she had to be really dressed up. But she had to change her plans before she left the house; I guess I changed her entire life from the day I was born. I walked by her side trying to keep up with her and I was always afraid to loose her. Since I was her shadow she made me learn that I had to keep my distance from her and her boyfriends.

One or two men at a time would come to our small two-room house; I would hide because I did not want to hear much less see those drunken wild perverts. Through the years when we were working after one of her wild parties she looked more lost and lonely than ever before. She had an angry, empty look and would work like an over powered robot, cleaning houses. I helped when I could but a couple of times on the way home she left me behind for and hour or so. I later found myself crying along a main street, talking to a man, I asked him if he had seen my mother. I had lost her at a corner store when we turned and she just left me there. When I came out of the store a man was there and he told me not to go anywhere until my mom came back for me. We waited about 45 minutes than my mom appeared. He tried to talk to her but she was angry and just told me to follow her. The second time maybe two or three months later when she got "lost" again; I just sat there where she had found me the first time. After that I understood that I should become invisible and out of my mother's way until she could stand to have me around her. I could not forget that man's look on his face and how he asked me "Is that your mom?" I proudly said "yes"! With a frown on his face he said "I would never claim her as my mom but that is not your fault."

By the age of seven or eight I had become very withdrawn and observant. My aunt Socorro once told me that when I was four years old my mother we moved away from them. She moved somewhere to San Juan about forty-five minutes away. My aunt told me this because I told her I had this memory of going next door to this lady' house several times, I asked her if she could find my aunt Socorro. The kind woman asked my name but I gave her my aunt's last name. I told her we were living in San Benito before coming there, my aunt came; much to mom's objections. My mother did not like living in the same town with my aunt and uncle, she did not like to be told what to do. I did not have any friends because most boys and girls teased me after six kids beat me badly. I had gone outside one day to test ride a tricycle my mom had gotten from somewhere. I had crossed the street which as off limits to me; I was really having a first fun time by myself. Then the oldest 14 year old boy came and threw the bike on the pavement and the others formed a circle around me.

I was on ground and my tricycle was on top; I was always wearing long skirts but now I was showing my legs. The oldest boy took one of the handle bars and pushed into my private part; my feet were being held down by the girl who enjoyed all the action. I struggled like I always did and the handle bar hit my left upper thigh. I was crying and screaming in pain when the girls' father came to my rescue. He ordered everybody home and he carried me to my house and handed me to my mom. I was in so much pain although the bar did not break my skin; it had deeply bruised a big part of my thigh. Mom did not take me to the doctor; she just kept me on my cot applying alcohol compresses. I remember being there a long time and not wanting to ever see that bike much less go outside, she agreed that I was safer by myself. I was terrified but I cried, hid under the cot and prayed myself to sleep every night.

I went to church with my aunt Socorro and asked Him to please take care of my mom and me. By the age of seven I was in deep conversation with God. Now I knew that He had always been there for me, we hurt but God always heals and rewards us. Than with His Grace we can develop independently and fly away. It was at this time that I remember I had been sick on and off but now it was worse. I must have been too much to handle so mom took me to my aunt's house. I did not know I could be so sick yet so happy! Happiness was united warmth and the perfect family, I begged God to keep me with my heaven sent family, but my mother had other plans. I could not understand why once every so often I had to go with her in one of her boyfriend's car. I did this until I was about ten, then this certain lady in the office made me very nervous. I was almost sure she had started all those strange people coming to the house. They asked all kind of questions but my mom and I got out of all the interrogations. It was at those times that I stayed with my aunt that I learned my life with her was better, peaceful, decent and productive. I learned that I could live honestly and eat right; my uncle was very responsible and my aunt very faithful. I had learned at four or five that it was going to be difficult for me to find food in the house. My mama would be off somewhere when I could not stand the hunger pains any longer. I walked during the early morning and I would gather the empty liquor or beer bottles. After the light liquid breakfast I would go back to sleep. Later I would wake up to my mother's screams she was always angry and in a hurry. I never knew her life style and drinking made her that way until I left home. She fixed something and often she sat down first, I could not wait to eat but at the end; I devoured everything on my plate.

Little did I know that I would be better off by myself! One of mom's friends "babysat me, she had about five kids the last one a newborn so at the age of seven I had to wash clothes on a washboard. My mother did not know any of this until two weeks later. When she came home I had burned my left hand and arm when I dropped a bucket of hot water. My mother took my to a neighbor's house after that; I was sleeping on the sofa when I felt someone touching me. He was a sixteen –year old male and his father was looking at him and laughing. When I was about six years old one of my mother's boyfriends was undressing me, he frightened me so much that I quickly jumped up and hit him right between the his legs. He fell down, moaned, vomit foam and crawled out the room. He never came back to mess with me after his third try and I now knew how to keep the enemy away. So now I put my secret hidden reflex to good use and for the second time it worked! These time though I quickly ran out the door about four in the morning. The next day my mother wanted me to go the babysitters' but after I told her what had happen she agreed that I was safer by myself.

I was about twelve and we still lived in the same barrio when Jose came to live with us. I liked him because he always went about his business with my mom, now we were a normal family and I was not afraid of him. All he would tell me was to run when I saw my mom ready to hit me; he defended me most of the time. I knew God had finally answered my prayers because my stepfather was very responsible and generous.

With no more housing or food hardships I studied harder than ever so I could graduate from school. Maybe I too, could be like my aunt! I saw how my aunt was decent, honest, loving and caring for her children and me. I swore to myself that I would rather kill myself if I had to sell myself or live like my mom. It was during one of these times in my life that I did try to slash my left wrist at about thirteen. But my mom found me and took care of my cut; no questions asked. Summers and weekends were the worst for me because my mom was always picking on me. At fifteen I took about eight of her pills and I remember sleeping a long, long time. Then she had me walking and forcing me to drink milk, screaming at me not to go back to sleep. I tried, but it was very hard to stay awake. When I did wake up two days had gone by and I was extremely pale and weak.

My dad and I were alike in a lot of ways; one was that we did not get too angry with my mom for the many things she did. First, when he got paid he would just give her all of his paycheck and immediately she wanted to go eat out to Matamorros. This was about 18 miles across the Mexican border; we went by ourselves on two occasions. But after they took her purse at the bus station; she decided it was better for them to go out dancing. I could not get angry because I did not have time to think negatively, I tried to survive and studied. My promise to God was never to hurt myself. I had learned at fifteen what self-destruction was! Lord forgive me!

My most positive and beautiful example in life was my aunt and uncle. He would sit in his favorite brown recliner and I was his favorite "puppy". I did not know what a puppy was until he told me to figure out the difference between a dog and a puppy. He said "go outside and find a big ugly dog and a small cute puppy." He was always sitting in his recliner and used to walk with a cane. It was not until I was about sixteen that I asked one of my cousins what was wrong with him and she replied flatly that he had an accident. I loved my uncle so much because I did not know a man could be so gentle, loving and so full of wisdom. I learned from my aunt how to worship God, do chores with pride and be pleasing to others.

With my mom the days ran into nights, without my knowledge. Some men would start coming to my house around four or five in the afternoon. I would feel nauseated at the sight of a particular imbecile at the tiny entrance of the kitchen. He was so familiar with the rest of the agenda to come. They were all wild and out of control. Everybody in there mostly my mom and two men would be so bad. Their animal instinct gave me nightmares. I remember taking a peek in there when I was about five and after that, learned a good lesson. I slept with my clothes so those men would not come at me. To this day I do not have any anger towards my mom or hold a grudge. I figured that she had to raise me the only way she knew. I survived and here I am!

But going back to my aunt and cousins, two girls and three boys showed me how to laugh, play and trust. We played outdoors in the fresh air and sometimes my aunt would come outside. She would wear her patch work apron. She worked non-stop from dawn to dusk and always cooked for an army of ten. My other aunt in Monterey was the same. They were my role models. They all gave me the lost, gone childhood that we all should have and cherish. I owe all my best growing up days to them! It was even my middle cousin Rey that gave me my first nickname! He called me "Matatoni" and when I asked him what it meant he replied "little killer". I felt so privileged that I had to go tell my uncle Lupe. He was watching television so I just sat next to him and enjoyed this marvelous invention that I had never seen before. It was just the two of us watching the big screen and then falling asleep in front of it. I woke up and now he was still asleep so I just sat there. After a while he woke up and said make me "piojito" so I can really wake up? I looked at him so confused that he was laughing so hard; he shook and asked, "Well, what are waiting for?" Feeling a little out of respect, I replied, "you are all bald headed where do I pick the piojitos" (lice)? He answered, "They are lying there just rub hard enough and you will find them". Now I could show him my gratitude and love. I did this every chance I had. The earth kept moving and we traveled and learned together. I can say that he was the grandfather I never had. I sure miss him! It was now that I had remembered my question so I proudly stood in front to him. Can you please answer a question, he said "girl you ask all the questions here for everyone including me!" I asked, "Is that good or bad?" He wanted to laugh, but did not and said "so what is the question?" I asked, "Do you like my nickname "Matoni"? He replied, I do not know and who named you that?" Feeling a little worried I said, "Rey," "Go get, Rey" he ordered! Oh my God, now I knew I did ask too many questions. There was Rey standing very handsome and straight then my uncle asked "why did you nick name her?" He answered "because dad we play little killers and cops; she is a girl killer ". My uncle said, "Well, it does not make much sense. But if it keeps her from asking any more questions it is okay". Before he finished the sentence we walked out faster than ever before and as for me I stop asking questions. I had been praying that I could please keep my heaven sent family when my uncle asked "FloRinda, why are you so sad?" My tears ran down my face. It hurt so much to see my uncle not being able to move. He was the first, gentle and generous giant I looked up to. Now he looked sad and held out his arms fighting back his tears. I told him "I hope you like me as much as I like you and I hope I never make you mad." He answered in his own witty manner "oh, I like you the same and you and nobody here has seen me mad." I can still feel that big, warm and gentle hug that only that smiling, humble, loving giant could give! My mother was always too busy, drunk or angry that she did not know how to hug much less say I love you. Now with the giant's arms caring for me I knew God does answer prayers although He sure took His time. Now I was about eleven on this particular hot summer cotton picking day. I was so annoyed that I picked harder to get away from the insults. There was a certain girl who lived in front of me and today she was picking next to me. When we were at home she would stand and scream insults from across the street. Her mother sat there and told the dumb girl what to scream at me. Today it was different she was next to me. She told me one insult after another for a good two hours. She had carried on far enough and I was totally exhausted. With my cotton sack three quarters full, I straightened up, took off my sack and faced her with a mean sun burned look. She was clapping her hands, jumping up and down. She knew that she had finally gotten to me! I grabbed her and fell to the ground on top of her. I was even hitting her in the face! People were running and screaming at me to leave her alone; I got up to drink water. The water could not cool the big murderer instinct I had displayed! Lord, I had not planned this and here I was. At eleven, I already was a convict and I never wanted to hurt anybody. Those famous tears ran down my face once again! The tears and sweat were all

I had to heal my hurt. I picked cotton all day without any food or water. This was my way of punishing myself; my next new home would be prison. We got home about seven almost every night. Quickly but not soon enough I heard my mom screaming for me at the front screen door. She had missed the live, lightweight wrestling match that day because both she and the other mom had stayed at home. When I got to the door, my mom yanked me by my ponytail and asked, "Did you really almost kill this woman's daughter today, instead of picking your one hundred pounds?" I answered, "only a little bit." The woman screamed through the screen "a little bit, you could have killed her"! My mother yanked my ponytail so hard that for sure now I knew I was bald, she asked why you did it. "Well I did pick two hundred pounds and I always mind my own business. Today she got next to me, but not to pick cotton "I pounded! Before my mother got a hold of my ponytail I moved back, now she had my arm and asked, "What did she do that was so bad?" I replied "she never shuts up, calls you a prostitute and everything else that she hears the others call you!" Now I was on the floor after being very implicit. I really did not even know what that unending word meant. I got up only to see my mom opening the screen door and points in the woman's face. My mom said "go file a complaint on FloRinda or whatever you please. I will bail her out either way." The woman started to say something but my mother said, "Now you need to go or I will file charges on you." After my first and last infamous incident that summer, I spent the whole, hot, lonely summer by myself. The injured damsel got lucky because she stayed the whole unbearable summer indoors which was nothing new. She would get in the truck not to go pick cotton but to have fun and meddle in other's business. This ongoing season turned into my most wisdom earned summers than all the others... After a few days of hard picking we went to eat our tacos for lunch. I already knew I had to look for my Dad who had everything ready to eat but I took another one of my inquisitive detours. Instead of going to eat I wanted to see what that weird smell came from so I followed it. It was some happy fellow smoking away and I was feeling just as happy but very nauseated. I turned around and started to run back to my safe haven. This one wild guy started to run in another direction. He ran after the crop dusting plane; the harder he ran the more he took in the fumes. I never saw him again after that dreary day. Every one else and I knew that cotton picking season was a way to save money. We had money saved for back to school and sometimes even the winter. The following summer I went to pick with my cousins and Baldemar Huerta, better known as Freddie Fender. He took his guitar and had his dream. I would hear him sing and thought life was good to all. We just had to live our lives in His likeness and grace to succeed.

We started another school year and I was so happy because I would be just my ordinary person again. Well, I had a great day at school but once I got home, another home dilemma on the street! My mom was screaming at the police in Spanish and all our belongings were outside. I fainted but I was again disconnected from my entire body. I was heavy and I couldn't walk; I just stood there my face wet with those famous tears. I managed to hug my mom who just dropped to her knees shouting obsencenties to everybody. Later I found out that my mom's boyfriend had died and he didn't put the house in her name. He was a very nice man but he was also married, so my mom was in deep loss and so was I.

I did not have any friends but I prayed endlessly to God that I made one with a little advice and a listening ear. At sixteen my prayer was answered again. My first, best and only friend came along. She had been living right at the corner of my house. I had to walk to Junior and High School than her older sister got a car. When they saw me walking to the ninth grade they stopped the car. My beloved friend got down and graciously asked if I wanted a ride? I almost exploded with emotion! That started our four-year friendship. Not too many people liked my mom or me; I just kept our friendship on the way to and from school. I could not mess up this opportunity. We graduated and I was able to go to Senior Day at Padre Island. My stepfather persuaded my mom to let me go. I think Jose; (my stepfather) was more considerate because he did not know how

to read or write when he came to live with
us. By my graduation day, I had taught him
how to sign his name read numbers and add
a little. His goal was to get his driver's license
and at forty-nine years, he got it! I went with
him and explained to the Highway Patrol
Officer that if he were given the written test
orally, Jose would answer in Spanish. Jose
barely but proudly got his license because
of the oral test. The driving test was easy;
he had been across the United States driving
loaded cargo just by following the leader
and faithfully praying to God all the way. He
would say that he never knew where he was
going but as long as there was work to do it
was God's calling. It was at about this time
when I was sixteen going on seventeen that
I drove his 1963 Buick and followed him.
He was driving his old Studebaker truck. I
did not have a driver's license and did not
drive. He needed someone to drive both his
vehicles because the other migrant families
had three or four children and supplies.
We traveled from Harlingen to Hereford
Texas, resting after six hours to have a three-
hour break. When we got there, the potato
packing company had small apartments for
all the families. We unpacked our clothes,
bedding and pots and pans. The men would

go immediately to the packing company so we could start to work as soon as possible. We stayed there all the summer and returned home about two days before school started. Sometimes three or more families migrated to Albuquerque, New Mexico. But my stepfather would not hear of it. He took us home and than returned to work by himself. That was my first summer working away from home and I was so happy because I was not working in the fields. I also had met a lot of nice people some my age. There was an older one of them named Lee. I had even been to a mall although I felt so much out of place. I walked home by myself because my neighbor's daughter was determined to sleep there if she could. I started school again but my mother was more determined to keep me working. I was in a lot of pain with my monthly periods. I could not tell her because when I approached her about it she hit me. She said that I was no longer clean. I did not say anything but I woke up the next day in a clinic with an IV. My mother was sitting next to me. I asked her what had happened and she replied that I had passed out. The doctor came in and said I was anemic and needed further medical care. Immediately my mom ordered that she was taking me home. My aunt happened to visit us after that. She always did when she had this motherly instinct about me; we talked in spite of my mom's rudeness. My aunt told my stepfather to cook calf liver and that would help through this. It must have been her prayers more than the liver; I made a remarkable recovery. I was now getting my diploma. I wanted to go to the Senior Prom but my mom said it was a waste of time and money. I settled for two graduation pictures and Senior Day at South Padre.

My goal was still in me and now I looked into Southmost College in Brownsville. Somehow I was immediately admitted and I told my Dad. He said that was the ultimate and I hugged and kissed him. "You are the ultimate" I said as he walked to his car. "Wait about one hour and see if I am the same". I was very worried and I asked "why"; he gave me a sad look and said "I am going to sell some of my blood to pay for groceries". "I have some money from my job." "No, no you are going to need every penny for college" replied my father. Now once again God had given me my own and best father and friend!

I graduated and I wanted to go to college but my mom said we were going to Hereford to work. I was once again so depressed I had a diploma but now what? We went to Hereford, Lee an older divorced man who was a workaholic like my dad met us at the apartments. In August of 1989, that we were working and I was very embarrassed because my mom was cursing me up and down loudly. She did this in front of everybody because we had worked long hours and we still had to go home and cook. I was used to her, but lately it was getting to me. The only thing I could figure out was that she physically or mentally did not feel good. I ran to the car and just started crying hysterically; my stepfather told her that she was really out of line. There in front of everybody at work she cursed him out too. I could not go on but at times like this I just worked harder to make time go by faster. I was in the kitchen when I heard my dad and mom fighting outside. She limped into the dining room and fell on the floor. I ran to help her but she was trembling and sweating. My stepfather and I put her in the car and took her to the emergency room. The doctors said she had a mini stroke but she was in there three weeks. Lee was the only other visitor that came to see my mom. One day he asked what I was going to do when I returned home. I said "the same thing" than he took my hand. He said "I love you very much and I am a lot older than you but I promise to make you happy. I took my hand away from his and laughed in his face. Why was I so cruel? He kept his visits to my mom. On one of those occasions he told my mom how he felt about me. Everybody was surprised to hear my mom say that Lee was a good match! All that summer I had been Lee's timekeeper and with the reports he had written me beautiful poetry. I treasured them and I never told anyone about it. Lee never gave up and we crossed the state line to be married in Clovis, New Mexico. After the wedding I brought my mom and brother back home. While I was there I went across the border to Reynosa to buy my wedding gown. When I got back to New Mexico in Lee's car and another migrant family he had talked to a Catholic priest. We had a big wedding in a small church in the Santa Fe Mountains. The altar was filled with white gladiolas and lit with lots and lots of candles. I never imagined Lee had such romantic, fairy tale ideas until that day. We danced all night at the old frame town meeting hall

and a local country live band played until
the following morning. I thanked Lee for the
storybook wedding that I had never even
thought about. I never even dated or had
a boyfriend. He answered, "We all should
have our dream wedding because it is for a
lifetime."

My life with Lee was full of questions
once again and I felt he had all the answers.
He would be there for me every time like
on the day he offered his services to my dad
and me. I had so many questions to ask Lee
that I started writing them down while he
was at work. We lived in New Mexico until
that Christmas and than we went to live
in Omaha, Nebraska. I wanted to go but I
asked him if it was going to be different than
living in New Mexico. I would never trade
those unforgettable days and nights in the
snow and the mountains. It was like I was in
a book living my true fairy tale with my very
own gentle giant. Lee took me to my first
night club and ordered the finest and most
expensive meal I had ever had. He would
buy me a new outfit for every occasion and
than pick a different restaurant. The first
time at this nightclub we even had men
playing violins at our table! I never knew

25

what to expect and Lee could only smile at my surprised look. He was getting used to me when I blushed and put my hands on my cheeks in amazement. Even on television I had never seen anything like this! That night the waiter asked what we would like to drink. I turned to Lee as I did for every thing and he ordered a little white wine. I was so glad that it was only a little glass because I really felt very happy now. He was laughing and said, "We are going to the movies you know?" I thought there were two or three of everything in that majestic club because that is what I saw. He said something like just not today. I could not talk just giggled. Slowly I walked like the lady that I was back to the car. Lee seemed a little concerned so he said we would stay in a hotel. It was about a ten-mile drive and there was a snowstorm. When we walked into the hotel I was again filled with curiosity and amazement. I asked why there were two beds. One even had a place to put coins in there. I would not give him a chance to answer all my questions. I saw the beautiful velvet curtains, the unreal view from the big windows I thought I was all a dream. He hugged me and asked if I liked our first night out together. I replied with a big hug and kiss. But before he did anything else I reached into pocket. Poor Lee, it was hard sometimes to stay ahead of me. I took out a handful of coins and asked him what to put in the slot by the bed. He grabbed a quarter and handed it to me I asked him "what do I do after I put the quarter in?" He said, "Maybe we should not do this." That only made me wonder why I should not do this so. I got on the bed and then put in the quarter. That bed started shaking sideways and sometimes I think it even moved up and down like it was possessed! I giggled and told Lee that was one of the best indoor rides next to the ferry wheel. Once the bed stopped and Lee regained his posture from laughing so hard he asked was I ready to call it a night. I replied "Oh yeah and what a night. The wildest in my entire twenty years!" I thanked my God, and acknowledged my blessing when I had my first son. Lee was a great husband, provider and father with the second birth of our son. Lee and I were married only eighteen short and unplanned years. So God, what do I do in my long and programmed years as a widow and single parent of two sons? Answer me Lord, I have been a good human being but this is one of my deepest losses! I did not know how to deaden my pain much less my sons' hurt. My oldest son was seventeen and the youngest eleven. Lee had told me that Thanksgiving morning when he was drank his coffee that his wish was to die just like that snapping his fingers. He died the Christmas morning after that Thanksgiving morning. I had reached for him in bed and he was gone. So I rushed to the kitchen and there he was all dressed up lying on the floor. He had a massive heart attack. I knelt down and felt his pulse without moving him. I called 911 and I whispered "do not leave me my love; I can not make it without you". He moaned deeply and I felt so useless. When the paramedics came I ran the get my oldest son. He only witnessed the inevitable and tragic loss. The paramedics took him to the hospital and I rode in the front. I kept asking myself why they don't turn on the siren. When we got there I waited a short time and than a doctor came in and asked "are you Mrs. Gamez"? I nodded and took his hand asking him "how is my husband?" "Ma'am he was dead on arrival" said the doctor. Without knowing I had been hurting the doctor's wrist. He yelled, "You are hurting my hand"! I let go and told him I was so sorry and cried until I thought I was numb. Finally the doctor asked, "What was your husband like?" I answered "he was a carpenter, always working, and a great sense of humor. He was never ill

Or in the hospital and no surgeries either." The young, kind doctor said" see how blessed both of you were. You had nothing but good, healthy and happy times. If your husband had lived be would be hooked up to machines and I do not know for how long." That Christmas we did not celebrate and I do not remember how long the tree was there. The void and emptiness grew with each passing day. The nights were so lonely and unbearable. Life had been marvelous with Lee and I still consider him my second best friend God being my first. I have talked to Lee about his sons and his precious five granddaughters sometimes. I still have those unforgettable memories and I live only the great past. I override all my sadness and depression and exchange them for motivation. My faith in God has strengthened me. I have stride with healthy anger to face all obstacles. I had persuasion and determination although I did not know. When Lee and I were going to Colorado on a new contract, again I began to contemplate the incredible snow and mountains that touched the sky. I stood there with snow up to my knees but I could not feel the cold. He came out and ordered me to get out of the cold. I was in a daze or in heaven! He came and hugged me and I said, "If I had not left my mom I would not be here. I did not know you very well but I just took my chances. I have seen so many of God's wonders and I never thought or planned it. It just happened!"

To my beloved late husband: December 21, 1988

To have known you was to have loved you. We pledged our love and we never forgot or broke our promise. Where are your thoughts, words and dreams now? Lee we shared everything and now you are gone like the wind. It was a very beautiful day, sunny but not hot or muggy. It was a bright, lazy, calm setting of our love, friendship and companionship that I just wish more of. I have stood there so many times saying out loud "okay, Lord you tell me what to do because you know me I can not do it by myself." I raised myself that way but with Lee around I had it so easy. Now it is back to my God and me.

My stepfather father died five years later after Lee also from a massive heart attack. I do not think my mom could cope with his death. Six months later her heart disease, diabetics and Alzheimer's was out of control. Now she is too weak and frail to be daring like when she was young and healthy. I ask myself when I visit her at the nursing home if she is still lost and lonely. Through her prime she traveled so fast and unproductive that now is too slow to hold a pleasant and dear memory. I asked her when I was about fourteen years old why she disliked me so much. She replied "because you took away my freedom. I used to be a care free spirit and do what I wanted." Those cold tears ran down my face and all I could reply was "I was born when you were thirty-two years old. That is now too bad." She had left the room shaking her head and mumbled something. When I have sat with her I only hope that she has asked God for her salvation. I have asked for all of us but I have always believed that we have to do own petitions. I have prayed and fasted many times and the blessings and prayers are answered.

I have always asked God to help me be a good mother but I know I made a very serious one. Two years later after Lee died I remarried and to this day I regret it. We went to Monterrey to meet the new in-laws. I also saw my other aunt and cousins that I had not seen in about thirty years. My aunt was eighty -six old and frail so I promised to come back with my mom. My mother and I had to go six months later because my aunt was barely hanging on. It was before Christmas of 1995, forty-five degree weather and beautiful snow covered mountains overlooking the bus station. We got out of the bus and I froze in deep thought. Were those the same mountains that Lee had taken me to? Then I got down contemplating and then playing in that white wonder. My mother said something and pulled me at the arm. I told her not to do that and we took another bus to my aunt's house. I did not feel good even before I left work for the holidays. By the time we got to my aunt's house I had a high fever. We visited with my aunt who was very ill and I told my cousin that I needed to go to sleep. She said, "You do not feel good do you?" touching my forehead. I just stood there and she said she would make me some green tea. I was sleeping when someone was putting a cold compress on my forehead. I did not know this woman and so I sat up asking 'who are you?" She replied "I am your aunt Lupe". She handed me a cup and I started to drink the tea. She sat at the edge of the bed. I really did not want any company but I did want to be rude either. She asked me" do have any children?" I replied flatly "two sons:" The older woman insisted "what are their names?" "Antonio Lee and Jaime Lee" I said looking at her rather annoyed. This woman persistently asked, "Why did you name your son "Antonio?"

I took a deep breath and said "if I tell you will you leave and let me sleep!" She nodded her head quiet embarrassed. I replied flatly "my father's name was Antonio and he died when I was little". The woman was standing with her hands clenched ready to say something. I said, "You said I could sleep now". She took a few steps back and than she said "your father is not dead". I demanded "how do you know?" She answered "because I work with him, he had a heart attack about five years ago and is in a wheel chair." My bad health and all the yearning for my father were too much for me. I had passed out and now my cousin was sitting next to me. I asked, "Do you know what that woman told me?" She nodded her head saying "and it is all true". I barely could get out the words "so why did not someone tell me; I always wanted to know what he was like!" I was crying helplessly when she hugged me and said "I am sorry but your mom threatened to never come back here if we told you about him". "My mother, my mother, when does she stop running my life! I am forty-three years old and all this time I could have known my father! I need to go see him. Do you know if he feels the same about me?" She and I had been very close since we were the same age and our mothers were sisters. Her eyes lit up and she said "you might but Aunt Lupe is the only one right now to tell you how and when you can go". I ordered with a smile "go, go and make sure she comes here right now!" Aunt Lupe came in and said "I am sorry if I upset you all this time I thought you knew about your father." I said "it is okay but I would like to go tomorrow to go see him. Will you take me?" "Well, first you must go see a doctor here because your father lives up in the mountains. We would take the three hour bus trip only if there is no danger of too much snow." I agreed nodding my head. The next morning I was going downstairs to the kitchen. There was my mom taking it out on my cousin. I took a deep breath and heard my mother say "I always did the right thing and you can be sure that after this I will never come back". I faced her and she asked me if I felt better. I stood there feeling colder than the brutal wind outside and said, "I would have felt better forty years ago! I got closer to her and continued "I had the right and privilege to know my father and you could not even let me have that! You do not know how many times I have wondered about him. What he looked like and if he even knew he had me." My mother kept eating and shut her ears to everything I had said like she always did. I got a cup of coffee and sat with my aunt until my cousin finished in the kitchen. About thirty minutes later my cousin and I walked to the doctor and he said I must return immediately back home. I could not believe my ears "why?" I asked. He said I had allergies but I had lived with it the last three years. My cousin said "but your blood pressure is also very high, please listen to the doctor". He gave me an injection and we walked the two blocks back to the house. I sat with my aunt Lupe and asked her about the travel conditions to the mountains. She nodded and replied "I am sorry but we can not go up there. I will have to stay here at least two more days." My cousin was sitting with us and informed my aunt what the doctor had ordered. "FloRinda, why do not you go home and on the first days of spring you come back and take your two weeks vacation here?" My cousin said, "That is the best idea ever!" I agreed since I felt weaker and I did not want to go back to their clinics or doctors anymore. After I got home I told my sons about my father, they too were very happy. I planned my two weeks' vacation and had my money saved for extra expenses. It was more than I had planned for; I was going to a beautiful place to meet my very own father! My father of forty-four years, my best birthday in Christmas! He was going to be my biggest Christmas present. I had not told my mother that I was going. After coming back from Monterrey I only visited her once or twice a week. She lived next door but I did not want to see her as often. She went on like nothing had happened. She never asked me anything or offered any explanation. My mom somehow found out that I was going to Monterey and was ready to tag along. I just ignored her most of the way. I had a bad feeling maybe because she was going or because I had been rude to her. I prayed on the bus and slept while we were in Texas. Once we were in Matamorros I had to be on my toes because one slight mistake and you could be extinct. Here we were and I looked for my aunt Lupe or my cousin, I spotted them and carried my baggage. I greeted them in a hurry because it was only ten in the morning; we could leave from there. My aunt Lupe insisted that we sit and talk. I told my cousin to take my mom with her. I felt my aunt take my hand and she said "FloRinda, wait there is something you have to know. I looked at her and I had this terrible numb void. I am so sorry but your father died." I had a ringing in my ears although the bus terminal was quite. I was a cold, stone pillar! It was about seventy degrees and sunny but I was frozen with disbelief. I do not know how long I sat there until I asked "when did he die and why did you not write to tell me?" My aunt answered "you remember that he had had a heart attack and he was in a wheel chair. About eight days ago he asked one of his ranch hands to help him on his horse. He loved to ride his horse although he was not supposed to. He had over two hundred acres in the mountains and decided to go there. They do not know if he had an accident, got exhausted or had another heart attack. They went to look for him that afternoon when he did not return. But it took five days to find him." My tears ran at forty-four intervals. My hopes and dreams were blown away in the cold wind. I have not gone back since and my poor cousin must feel bad. I have written her letters and they come back returned. She had a beautiful home and lived by herself.

Because she had a sister nearby she had thought about moving in with her. I never got my Aunt Lupe's address. Maybe one day I can gather more illusions so I can go back. I would only like a good picture of my dad. My aunt Lupe said he had two sons but one died when he was twenty-six in a truck accident. The other stayed at home and I was the oldest and only daughter. My aunt told me that he would ask my cousin about me and he knew that he was my father. My cousin said that his last wish was to see me. I could not answer her, but there in heaven he can know that I feel the same way.

It was about this time that I wrote the following when I thought about my sons. Your mother is that woman that gives you all her unconditional love, which is rare and hard to come by. This love is genuine, lasting, unpredictable and hopeful. The tough love that I have is one that I am still trying to nurture. My love for you is not perfect and neither is the intended path I took. I want to keep my sons away from the pain and mistakes that I made. I can only pray that God will give them the grace to walk good miles before they stumble. You will fall but you will get up stronger and wiser because

I did many times. This makes me a good mother but not perfect.

I feel like my lonely and hard childhood paved the way to my good life. How many people have suffered worse hardships in their upbringing and they are successful because of them. I have heard many of these stories even before I could tell mine. It was then that I realized I had been lucky because I had my aunt and her entire family to care for me. I was talking to a pastor one time and he said, "Do you know that no body knows how our lives will really turn out?" I immediately looked past that comment. Before I could ask him he continued "see God knew before you were born what you were up against. He knew everything because He was always there. He has a plan for everyone on this earth but our choices will determine what we want to do with our life." Boy, I was stuck to the church bench! I had heard this before but now it really had made an impact because I was on my own once again. I am on my own but my choices will affect my two sons and five granddaughters. Yes life is beautiful and plentiful. My granddaughters mean the world to me and they are my motivation and inspiration to each day. I am now grandma Flo and I always wanted a

Daughter. But God multiplied blessings with five precious granddaughters and a grandson!

Silly Grandchildren

I love you because you are so silly!

Do not be angry and but utterly dilly!

I like you silly, so bubbly and loud.

More than a big and bright cloud!

Your silly love is what warmth is to anguish.

Your love is what a song is to a sigh!

Your love is what a white dove is to a hawk.

My babies' smile soothes my throbbing pain.

My silly granddaughters reign though my years gain.

I love you, silly for giving me back my childhood.

I love you, silly for taking away my old chicken coop!

FloRinda alias Grandma Flo

I always considered myself so fortunate to have my sons, although I always wanted two sons and two daughters. My sons are both mine but oh so different! That is why I wanted two of each. An elderly and godly man once told me that he had six sons and six daughters. He said they were all different, but it was then that he found out Gods' purpose. He had put a lot of color and variety in his life and wonder through the children. My thoughtful, wise friend trying to sooth my new role of a widow and single parent then told me to look at my hands. He said "they are both yours and almost perfect but why were all fingers different sizes? He just smiled and said "you will do all right bringing up your sons by yourself. You just found another inner strength, your hands. Your faith in God is the first and the second your hands to pull your sons with you.

Now that I sit to admire my six beautiful grandchildren, I know that God is awesome! He blessed me with my privileged variety and wonder that not all of us have. I give

Him the entire honor and praise for genuine grandchildren, all so beautiful yet all so different! I could spend my all my older days just looking at them through my bifocals. With my gray hair and golden years I will be singing out their names over and over. I now have my answered, gigantic blessings in the slow, simple, peaceful and latter stage of my life. My grandchildren with their witty words and curios minds instill in me that gifted, positive energy that gives me an unforgettable day and a restful night's sleep!

Happy Birthdays, mis hijos!

To my sons, I have to tell you both the following before another year goes by in our lives. I have always wondered if it would be more difficult to have a daughter than a son. Now thanks to God and you I have found out. I am so privileged to have such beautiful grandchildren! Although I now think that it might be harder to have a daughter. I feel that you have a more over protective and sensitive love towards a daughter. Having been a girl a while back, I was somewhat delicate, sensitive and caring. That was on my good side, we all know my bad side. That is why now I have to hope that my granddaughters will be loved, cherished and well cared for. Men also need the same but I think women are more fragile.

My granddaughters are like my roses! They are lovely with that sweet aroma. They need to be watered with lots of love. For one day when they are in full bloom, they will take their scent and start their own growth. It is a special privilege to be your mother and have my answered privileges blooming! I thank God for my sons, granddaughters and roses!

Happy Birthdays, mis hijos,

Your ever-blooming mom

Lee,

I never knew how much you were in our lives until now. Lee, I can't talk to our sons much less talk to them like you could. God has been too good being there for us but why did He have to take you? I have tried so many times but I feel like I am not getting anywhere and you could talk with that charisma and concern that you had for everybody. I have asked myself even researched how to get across them, my sons not to mention my spouse and I have not succeeded. You could touch hearts in your sleep and it is a gift that not everybody has. I will keep on trying but I hope I can one day be just a good parent and see my rewards.

You would not believe how much joy and inspiration the grandbabies have brought into my life. I have made this far because there were many times I called it quits. Single parenting has to be the toughest job there is and even then I am now more selfish than ever before. I want to grow old even to see all of them in their early, settled and professional lives. Well, I mean who knows what the five granddaughters and Tony Jr. will be! Little Flo, alias Gabrielle, might one day be a lawyer. There is one problem with that she would be very grouchy, not to mention expensive. Gwendolyn Lee would make a good psychologist, successful one at that. Mia Lee worries me because she is too quiet to the point you don't know where she is coming from. I wish I could see the other three more because I don't. Your oldest son is not close with either his brother or me.

Lee, I am so lucky and privileged that it makes me sad that you, mom and dad were not so blessed like I am. I hurt to think that I could just watch you all meet with pride and laughter when those little ones say and do the silliest things. Yes, Lord I am a millionaire in my blessed and old age so much more that the real millionaires. Money does not buy all the amazement and unexpected calls from those grandbabies. I keep their calls and play them over and over just to hear their voices and laughter. I wish I could have all of your voices recorded too and play them over and over. I would play your voicemails and ringtones to my grandbabies so they could hear your soothing and calm tones. Money doesn't buy or download those beautiful memories I just treasure them in my heart. Rest my loved ones I will pray and thank my God for all my blessings and tell Him how thankful I am one more time.

I believe we all have a purpose in life. I am still trying to fulfill mine. With all my memoirs I hope I can especially touch all my loved ones and a few others. My mom had well in her although she led the life she did. I did not like her life style but it is good that we made it this far. I know others have been through worst so I can not complain. I got through life praying to God and always believing in Him. Many people say "well I do not know how to pray". More than twice I have said "it is just like talking to someone or even yourself". Oh, I am so blessed because I have it all. I just need to never let go.

PART 2
UNKNOWN FATHER
LOST MOTHER

My mother is gone and I find myself with a lot of free time and another big void. I got to see her seven or eight final days and nights and she didn't take those painful and heart wrenching memories with her. She chose to have no machines and no tube feedings which I was against but I had never told her what to do. I could only put ice chips on her cracked lips and later a wet sponge until she could no longer had the strength to take in. I wish my tears can soaked your hurting lips mom, instead your last two or three tears roll down your cheeks. Lord, she is hurting and when will it stop; she was all I had and now she is drying away. My mom had wonderful medical care but nobody ever knows what in store at our final earthly stay. She is gone and she looked beautiful in pink, she is in a better place.

With so much time on my hands I am writing and applying for a job even volunteer work. Anything to fill in the void and gap that I feel inside but it is not as easy as I thought. There is a big world out there and it all past by me when I cared for my mother those four years. I start working as a caregiver to an elderly lady who did not have any children and before you know it she too is gone. This has to stop just when I start loving and bonding I am left in limbo, the emptiness is mind bogging. My home life has also suffered because I have not been 100 0/0 for them maybe not even 50. Life has given me my two sons and six grandbabies so why don't I just try that for beginners? To my surprise life did not stop them and they all have a full schedule and lots of plans.

I am with my Tia Socorro she can use my always sweet and caring company so she says. The days here are very relaxed and non-stop at 89 years she has more vitality and energy than I do. "Why do you sleep so much is it because of all those pills you have?" I just smile and give her another tight hug and tell her I love her hell of a lot. She lets out a big laugh and says one more time you are more of a niece to me too and you my loving husband told me that too. I am not aware of another relaxed and beautiful day; I must go walking before sunset. Maybe this will be my retirement area growing up here was awesome. This is nice but I would have to change a complete way of lifestyle and my sons and grandchildren would be six hours away.

After a two stay I come back to my house and find the same old void I thought I had packed away in the lost luggage. It must be me and my yearning to belong and love again; I know I have the potential; where do I start, Lord please hurry and make me productive and able to support myself.

I am taking some basics at a junior college and even my thirteen year old granddaughter can learn faster. I got so overwhelmed and busy that I had a mini-stroke. During my ongoing schedule on my regular old routine I am now with the Domestic Violence Division. I see the insecure and lost faces of the mothers and children and my heart goes out to them. If I can't relate to this temporary arrangement these children are probably more sensitive than the adults. I thought I had been through it all when I was a child and I would escape into my own little safe world. Now I call my aunt every week sometimes twice a week to remind her how much I love her. It is once in our busy and regular lives that we forget how much we have and not appreciate it.

During this time I also ran into one of my old friends, she is very distraught because her granddaughter and grandson are off to war. We both cry, I could only let her pour out her heart. These are her only two grandchildren and they are gone. I thank God again for my family being together and pray that all those in the armed services can also be safe and hopefully return soon. This is the second time that I live through all the turmoil that the wars bring; the first being Vietnam. I was in high school and some of my friends were leaving right after graduation.

Times are hard and now I feel that I really have to make the best of it because I have endured so much. I look in the mirror and see a woman that has not lived through the present absence of her children and loved ones at war. I consider myself very fortunate and promise God that I will not soak in my self pity anymore. He brings many blessing in mysterious ways and once I opened eyes to those that are going through worst I am humble. Actually at one point I was selfish and stagnate in my own toxic world. Life is too short to waste it like that and not move on to the positive and bright lives we have.

I run into my godchildren they were newborns now they are 22 and 25. My oldest who is 35 and her six children came all the way from Florida to visit me. I am so lucky to be a part of their lives and this is when I know He always had me in His care and plan. Why did I waste precious time in petty feelings when I have so much to live for? Now I want to do my best that my health can take and be there for those that want to share their moments with me.

Today I ran into an acquaintance who asked about my sons and grandchildren. I said the usual and he said "you know I think I am really blessed because I never had any kids." I just stood there not knowing what to answer; he immediately parted and I kept on walking. Now I was thinking what a void and empty heart I would have if I was in his shoes. How can you be blessed without any offspring maybe because I never wanted to be alone? I have everything I always wanted and I can understand that some people choose to be single and or have no children. Life to me is being very family close knit forever no matter what downfalls come I will be there for them. There are change of the times but the family love we have will always be the same; everlasting and united. I am sitting outside my back patio and this particular red bird chirps away almost at

2pm everyday. He must do this to say hi or maybe it's his way of telling me how much I time I have done in my lost world. Who am I to have judged my mom as lost when I too, came close to closing all the doors to all the loves of my life? I was too depressed and absent letting precious hours slide through without any consideration for my young sons and beautiful grandbabies. No wonder this bird is still chirping away, he is going non-stop. He sure has a long list up his feathered wings.

It is when that red bird finally stops his song that I write the following

To know you is to love you, that is what you once said but now you have forgotten me. Why have you forgotten me and everything you once told me? Where are your thoughts, words and times we shared; all taken with you and the wind? It was a very beautiful day; sunny, but not muggy. It was a bright, lazy, calm setting. You said, "I love you'. I was surprised yet smiled and worried that I would jump with gratitude. Grateful to God for letting us find the best of friends, but I did not know you felt like I did! You have been my great friend, companion, and now you wanted to be my shadow.

What happened to that love and friendship we found? Did it get lost in the wind, heat or dark? NO, because it was a beautiful day! Now I am in the dark and it is a very, dreary and cold, cold summer day. You can love me, but do not overwhelm me with your unsecured, jealous and adolescent behavior. Let me make my own decisions and when I ask your opinion, be serious and do not degrade me with uncalled remarks. We have lost communication, not to mention the trust we had in each other. The consideration was blown away in the dark, the trust in the wind and the respect in the cold. To love me is to know me and not to change me; to love me is to respect me and not to do degrade me. I will in turn do the same with you; the same genuine person I met that beautiful, bright lazy and calm day.

This I had started writing one day when my late husband and I had a serious disagreement. We did not fight but this a serious encounter and now many years later I finally finished it. Writings like this always usually make me wish I had someone of my very own again.

I have lived alone and I have all the time to do as I please but I would like to have a companion that also needs my company. I have had some men ask me out but I always get very defensive and I end up scaring them off. I guess I will stay by myself but when I feel like company I end up reading a good book or writing. My granddaughters also visit along with my son and a have good friends and neighbors. I had three friends two that died from breast cancer and one that moved away. All of them were single and they said that they never had felt like getting married again. They were too set in their ways and could not change for anybody else. Now I guess I fill that criteria because I don't have any friends or plans to get one. Now I feel I can do what I always wanted to and not worry about tending or leaving anybody. I never imagine traveling, writing and seeing all the beautiful scenery out there.

I am going upstairs to see mom, the floor is heavy on my feet. Why is it I don't want to look at mom? She is so perfect, her eyes are closed but her mouth a little open just when she took her afternoon nap. I kiss her and she is colder than a frozen icicle she lets a deep painful moan. She is getting heavier and colder than her ice block frame; I am crying hysterically my mom has died in my arms. I thought I would be able to face this moment but how do I let go! Mom, I told you I loved you many times but only in the last year. We bonded together in the last four years of our entire lives, I still thank my God for the times you and I had. I get ready for another empty start to another dreary day and wouldn't you know it I am in mom's room. I throw her old rocker against the wall and I didn't put a scratch on it oh yea, but she could die and leave this life long dent in my heart. Mom, why did you always get your way? For your information I do feel guilty for wanting you to pay for all the times you left me alone and lost. Now that is in the least of my wants or needs, I just want you back in my life. Why do I feel like I am the one that is being punished one more time when I lose another love of my life?

Mom I never finished this until now I hope you can let me know from up there if you like it.

My mother, my friend, my companion and twin.

Is now my weak and frail child.

My mother, my silly child in the back seat of the car.

Too tired and ready for a nap!

My twin sister who borrowed my clothes, shoes or whatever she liked…with no intention of returning them.

My uninvited over-dressed companion even if I was "just going around the corner".

She was always there like my shadow.

My mother, my ever loving silly child, now growing old and too tired even to laugh at me when I reprimand her!

I was blessed to have such a mother that is why I held on to her.

But now I know my God's calling you. I must obey and respect our Master's will.

Her intravenous hour is finished and the alternative occurs.

I am seating in my mom's hospital room and I just wrote these thoughts; feeling so impotent and helpless!

I always carried my notebook and at times like these, that is all I could do cry and cry. I just fall in the chair again I am overworked, old restless and a lost nervous human being.

I will never understand or explain my mother's behavior but I can honestly say that I loved her and respected her as such. I only want to be a good mother and grandmother that my children will be proud of. I guess that goes for every parent and that was my goal in writing all my memoirs. I hope I can be of some help and inspiration especially to the single parent.

About the Author

With her memoirs she hopes she can especially tough the single parent and their children. She had a rough childhood but that probably led to a stronger survival towards an unpredictable future. She knew of the void and lost love that she grew up with when neither parent was there for her.

In "Unknown Father Lost Mother" she tells the story of her childhood growing in San Benito, Texas. She reflects on growing up without a father and living with her drawn and absent mother. She writes about the time when her mother gets "lost" and leaves her alone and hungry. Gamez describes her mom's boyfriend's attempts to touch her when they came to visit her home. She learns to have deep conversations with God and plea for His guidance and assistance. Gamez expresses her love for her deceased husband children and above all God. On whole and common theme told throughout the book is that of her faith in God and waits for His salvation for her and all her loved ones. Now a grandmother of six, Gamez is in privileged and cherished wonderland where her beautiful and witty grandbabies reign!